# Herbivores

Jill Foran

WEIGL PUBLISHERS INC.

Published by Weigl Publishers Inc.
350 5th Avenue, Suite 3304, PMB 6G
New York, NY 10118-0069 USA
Web site: www.weigl.com

Library of Congress Cataloging-in-Publication Data

Foran, Jill.
  Herbivores / Jill Foran.
      p. cm. -- (Nature's food chain)
  Includes index.
  ISBN 1-59036-240-3 (lib. bdg. : alk. paper) 1-59036-264-0 (pbk.)
  1. Herbivores--Juvenile literature.  I. Title. II. Series.
  QL756.5.F67 2004
  591.54--dc22

                                    2004012602


Printed in the United States of America
1 2 3 4 5 6 7 8 9 0   08 07 06 05 04

**Project Coordinator** Janice L. Redlin  **Design and Layout** Bryan Pezzi
**Copy Editor** Don Wells  **Photo Research** Simon Daykin

**Photograph Credits**
Every reasonable effort has been made to trace ownership and to obtain
permission to reprint copyright material. The publishers would be pleased
to have any errors or omissions brought to their attention so that they may
be corrected in subsequent printings.

**Cover:** koala bear (**Photos.com**); **CORBIS/MAGMA:** pages 8L (Enzo & Paolo
Ragazzini), 8R (Enzo & Paolo Ragazzini); **Corel Corporation:** page 5R; **Digital Stock
Corporation:** page 15B; **PhotoSpin Inc.:** page 14B; **Photos.com:** pages 1, 3, 4, 5T, 5L,
5M, 5B, 6, 7T, 7B, 9T, 9B, 10, 11T, 11B, 12, 13T, 13B, 14T, 15T, 15M, 18, 19T, 19B, 20TL, 20TM,
20TR, 20ML, 20MM, 20MR, 20BL, 20BM, 20BR, 22.

**On the Cover:** The koala bear has a large nose with a good sense of smell. The nose
helps the koala choose good quality eucalyptus leaves.

All of the Internet URLs given in the book were valid at the time of publication.
However, due to the dynamic nature of the Internet, some addresses may have
changed, or sites may have ceased to exist since publication. While the author
and publisher regret any inconvenience this may cause readers, no responsibility
for any such changes can be accepted by either the author or the publisher.

# Contents

# Nature's Food Chain

All living things need food to survive. Food provides the energy that plants and animals need to grow and thrive. Plants and animals do not rely on the same types of food to live. Plants make their own food. They use energy from the Sun and water from the soil. Some animals eat plants. Others eat animals that have already eaten plants. In this way, living things rely on each other and form a food chain.

A food chain is made up of **producers** and **consumers**. Plants are the only producers in the food chain. This is because they make energy. This energy can be used by the rest of the living things on Earth. The other living things are called consumers. There are four different types of consumers in a food chain. They are herbivores, carnivores, omnivores, and decomposers. All of the world's animals belong to one of these consumer groups. The first level of consumers in the food chain is called herbivores.

Bees have enlarged hind feet that often have baskets made of stiff hairs used for gathering pollen.

## Did you know?

If an animal's food source disappears, other animals will suffer and possibly die.

# Food Chain Connections

The Sun

Decomposer (consumer)

Omnivore (consumer)

Carnivore (consumer)

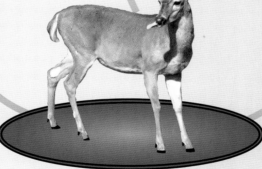

HERBIVORE (consumer)

Plant (producer)

# What is a Herbivore?

*Herbivore* means "plant eater." It is a Latin word. The term herbivore describes animals in the food chain that only eat plants and **vegetation**. Herbivores get their energy from eating plant materials. This can include flowers, fruit, grasses, leaves, and even wood. They are able to **digest** the plants they eat. Then they convert the energy in the plant cells for their own use. Some examples of herbivores include deer, elephants, and rabbits. Most insects and many types of birds are also plant eaters.

Rabbits feed on a wide variety of shrubbery and vegetation. They are often responsible for small and thin growth of ground cover.

The diets of herbivores vary. Some herbivores feed on only one type of plant. Others eat all kinds of vegetation. Many herbivores do not have to look hard for their food. For example, cows are usually surrounded by the grasses they need to eat to survive. Other herbivores must work harder to find food and survive. In the world's **temperate** zones, herbivore diets depend on the season. This is because different plant foods grow during different times of the year. In the spring, they might eat the tender shoots or growths of blooming plants. In the winter, they eat the bark of bare trees.

Calves drink their mother's milk early in their lives before switching to eating grass and other vegetation.

Did you know?

Monophagous herbivores eat only one kind of plant. The koala bear is a monophagous herbivore. It eats only eucalyptus leaves.

# Built for Plant Eating

All herbivores have features that are **adapted** to their diets. Many herbivores have special body parts that help them chew and digest plant material.

Among the most important body features for all herbivores are the teeth. These teeth are designed for eating vegetation. Herbivores that gnaw at plants have sharp **incisors** for cutting through nuts, wood, and other thick plant material. Herbivores that grind their food before swallowing, such as caribou or deer, have flat **molars** for grinding their meals.

Examine the photos of a carnivore's teeth and a herbivore's teeth. What differences do you see?

## Comparing Animal Jaws

Carnivore jaw (crocodile)

Herbivore jaw (kangaroo)

Cows have four chambers in their stomach instead of just one. When a cow swallows grass or other plants, the food goes to the first chamber, called the rumen. There, bacteria breaks the food down into something called cud. Later, when the cow is resting, the cud is sent back to the mouth to be chewed again. It is then swallowed into the other three stomachs. This process makes digestion easier.

Bison mostly eat during the day. Their diet consists of bark from a variety of bushes and grass, leaves, trees, and twigs.

Other herbivores with similar stomachs include antelope, bison, deer, and sheep. Mammals with more than one stomach are called **ruminants**.

### Did you know?

The jaws of many herbivore mammals move from side to side instead of up and down. This helps these animals grind and crush tough plant material.

# Birds and Beaks

Many different kinds of birds are herbivores. Herbivorous birds do not have teeth. Instead, they use their beaks to eat. Some birds, such as the hawfinch and the parrot, use their short, strong beaks to open nuts and seeds. Their beaks act much the same way that a nutcracker works.

Sapsuckers do not crack nuts with their beaks. These birds eat the sugary sap out of trees. They use their long, sharp beaks to dig holes in trees and draw the sap out.

**Parrots have strong feet with two toes in front and two in back. The feet help them climb and grasp branches while they eat the fruits and seeds of trees.**

Another type of herbivorous bird is the hummingbird. This tiny bird drinks the sugary **nectar** found deep inside flowers.

When a hummingbird is eating a meal, it uses its beak, tongue, and wings. It pokes its long, thin beak into a flower and stretches out its tongue. The tongue acts like a straw and sucks the liquid out of the flower. As the hummingbird drinks, it hovers over the flower by flapping its wings very quickly. Hummingbirds are the only birds that can fly backward and sideways, as well as forward.

A hummingbird's feet are too weak to support its weight on flat surfaces. It must hover over a flower when feeding.

### Did you know?

Most birds have a special muscular portion in their stomach called a gizzard. The gizzard helps birds to digest food. It crushes and grinds grains, hard nuts, and seeds. Some birds may also swallow small stones and gravel. This can help the gizzard grind and crush.

# Millions of Insects

Insects are the largest number of herbivores. There are more insects in the world than all other forms of life put together. Scientists have identified more than 1 million insect **species**. Today, there are millions more insect species that have not yet been discovered. Many species of beetles, flies, grasshoppers, moths, and snails are plant eaters.

Large swarms of migratory grasshoppers, including locusts, feed on crops, such as barley, corn, oats, rye, and wheat. They take only a few hours to damage an area.

One of the most beautiful insect herbivores is the butterfly. Different species of butterfly are found around the world. Most butterflies thrive in warm, tropical climates. They feed on nectar from flowers. They also drink the sweet juice from ripe fruits. A butterfly uses its tube-like tongue to sip its meals. This tongue is called a proboscis. A butterfly unfolds the proboscis to sip the nectar. When the butterfly finishes drinking, it rolls its proboscis underneath its head.

Some butterflies are known to migrate toward the equator for the winter. Flowers and fruits are more plentiful in these warmer climates.

## Did you know?

All butterflies start their lives as eggs. A butterfly usually lays its egg on a leaf. Soon, a caterpillar hatches from the egg. As the caterpillar grows and changes, it eats. Some caterpillars will only eat the kind of plant on which they were born.

# Herbivore Closeup

There are many different kinds of herbivores. They come in all shapes and sizes. Some of the world's largest and smallest animals are herbivores. Herbivores can be found in different parts of the world. Some of them live in bodies of water. Many of them live on land.

## Elephant

- largest land mammal
- lives in **savannah** grasslands and rain forests
- muscular trunk picks up objects and rips branches from trees
- tusks are incisor teeth; teeth are replaced up to four times in a lifetime
- eats bark, grasses, and leaves

## Green Iguana

- can be as long as 6 feet (2 meters)
- lives in the tropics and subtropics of Central and South America
- is arboreal, which means it lives in trees
- its **dewlap** regulates body temperature
- eats mostly leafy greens that are high in calcium

# Giraffe

- tallest mammal
- lives on the grassy plains of Africa
- long neck enables it to eat from tall trees
- can stretch its tongue more than 17 inches (43 centimeters) to get food
- mostly eats the leaves and twigs of acacia trees

# Snail

- most snails are herbivores
- lives in fresh and salt water and in moist land areas
- has a soft body protected by a hard shell, which it retreats into when threatened
- garden snail is the slowest-moving animal
- eats living and decaying plants

# Manatee

- is 10 feet (3 m) long and weighs 1,200 pounds (544 kilograms); never stops growing
- lives in fresh and salt water in Central, North, and South America
- new teeth grow at the back of its mouth
- eats over 150 pounds (68 kg) of food each day
- eats manatee and turtle grass, water hyacinth, and water lettuce

**15**

# Herbivore Habitats

All herbivores require special living conditions in order to thrive. The place where an animal lives is called its habitat. Earth has many different habitats. A herbivore's habitat can be as big as a desert or a forest. It can also be as small as a tree branch or a pond. Each herbivore must live where it can get the food it needs to survive. For example, zebras rely on grasses to get their nutrients. They would not live long in the forest.

Some of the world's largest habitats include deserts, grasslands, temperate forests, tropical rain forests, and tundra. Look at the map to see which types of herbivores live in each of these habitats. Can you think of other herbivores to add to each of the habitats?

Herbivores in the tundra: caribou, arctic hares, lemmings, squirrels, voles

Herbivores in tropical rain forests: butterflies, parrots, sloths

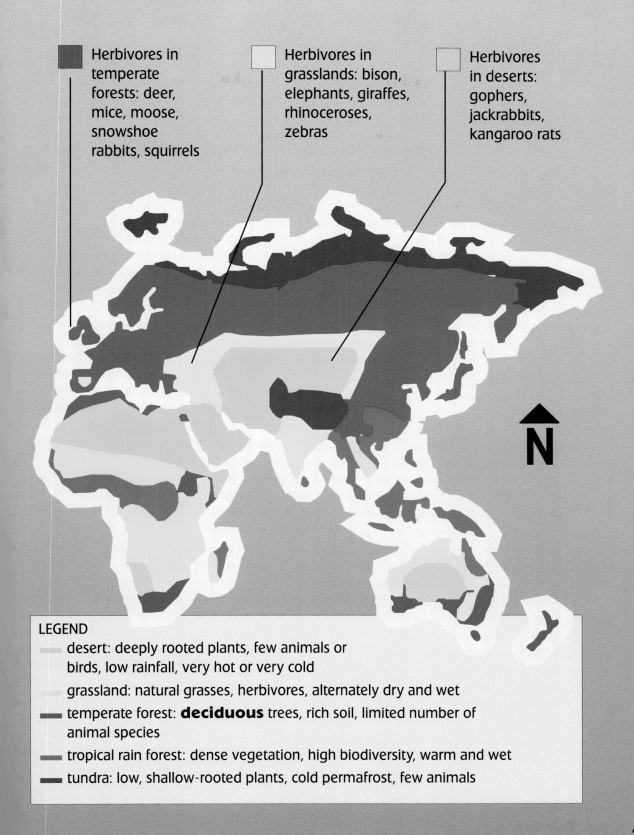

Herbivores in temperate forests: deer, mice, moose, snowshoe rabbits, squirrels

Herbivores in grasslands: bison, elephants, giraffes, rhinoceroses, zebras

Herbivores in deserts: gophers, jackrabbits, kangaroo rats

**N**

LEGEND

— desert: deeply rooted plants, few animals or birds, low rainfall, very hot or very cold

— grassland: natural grasses, herbivores, alternately dry and wet

— temperate forest: **deciduous** trees, rich soil, limited number of animal species

— tropical rain forest: dense vegetation, high biodiversity, warm and wet

— tundra: low, shallow-rooted plants, cold permafrost, few animals

# Herbivores at Risk

Plants and animals rely on each other in order to survive. For example, many birds and mammals eat the fruits that fall from forest trees. These animals then drop the fruits' seeds. The seeds sprout into new plants. In this way, animals help to make new plants grow. Bees use **pollen** from flowers as food. As they collect pollen, they spread it from flower to flower. Many plants cannot grow unless they are **cross-pollinated** by bees or other insects. If there were no flowers, bees would die. If there were no bees, many plant species would die.

In the United States in the 1980s, farmers rented bees from beekeepers to pollinate their crops. Pesticide use had greatly reduced the bee population.

When a herbivore's habitat is destroyed and food is no longer available, that herbivore becomes **endangered**. Every day, herbivores, from insects to mammals, become endangered or **extinct**. An endangered herbivore puts carnivores and plants

at risk, too. In most cases, humans cause the world's plants and animals to become endangered. When people clear land to build communities or grow crops, many plants and animals lose their homes and their food supplies. Some environmental groups work to preserve the world's natural habitats.

The growth of new plants on cleared land occurs very slowly. It can take many years for the vegetation to grow back.

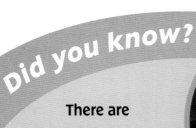

Did you know?

There are more than 600 endangered species of animals in the United States.

# Making a Food Chain

Plants and animals are linked together through food chains. In this way, all living things depend on one another for survival. Each one of the herbivores in the pictures is part of a unique food chain. Look closely at these herbivores. In what type of food chain do these animals belong? What does the animal eat? What animals eat it?

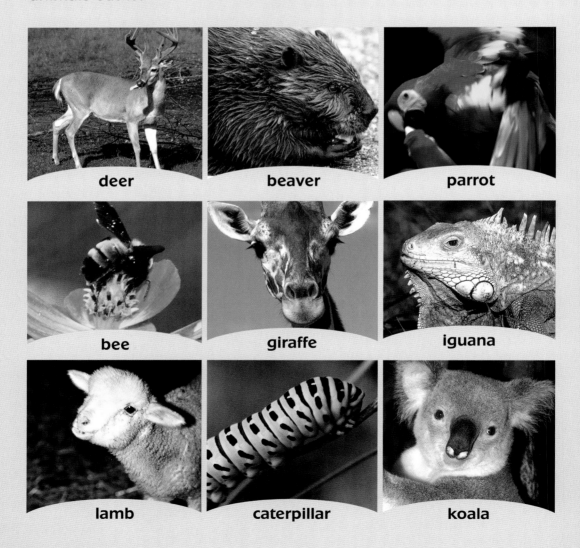

deer     beaver     parrot

bee     giraffe     iguana

lamb     caterpillar     koala

Once you have examined all of the pictured animals, pick one and learn more about it. Using the Internet and your school library, find information about the animal's diet. Explore which carnivore or omnivore might eat it. Draw a picture of a food chain that illustrates what you learned. If the herbivore you chose belongs to more than one food chain, create more than one. Write an explanation about why the herbivore does or does not belong to more than one food chain.

Do you have any pets that are herbivores? Is there anybody in your family or school who is a herbivore? If so, write something about what the herbivore eats. What special features does its body have that assists it in eating?

**One example of a food chain starts with a plant (producer). Large animals, such as giraffes (herbivores), live on plants. Giraffes are eaten by consumers. Energy is transferred from one living thing to another in a food chain.**

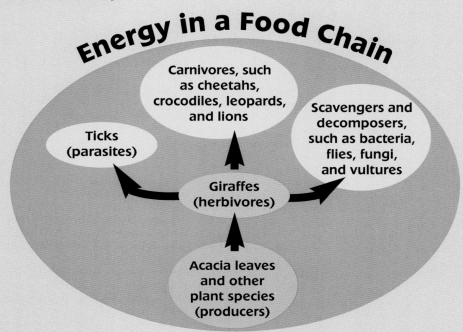

## Energy in a Food Chain

Carnivores, such as cheetahs, crocodiles, leopards, and lions

Scavengers and decomposers, such as bacteria, flies, fungi, and vultures

Ticks (parasites)

Giraffes (herbivores)

Acacia leaves and other plant species (producers)

# Quiz

**Based on what you have just read, try to answer the following questions correctly.**

1. What does the word herbivore mean?

2. What is the tallest herbivore on Earth?

3. What is another name for a butterfly's tongue?

4. How many stomachs does a cow have?

5. What do hummingbirds eat?

6. Are plants considered producers or consumers in the food chain?

7. What is a monophagous herbivore?

8. What herbivore is considered the largest land mammal in the world?

**Answers:** 1. Plant eater 2. The giraffe 3. Proboscis 4. Four 5. Nectar from flowers 6. Producers 7. A herbivore that eats only one kind of plant 8. The elephant

# Further Research

There are many more interesting facts to learn about the world's herbivores. If you are interested in learning more, here are some places to start your research.

## Web Sites

To learn more fascinating facts about herbivores, visit:

**www.nhptv.org/natureworks/nwep9a.htm**

To learn more about herbivore habitats, visit:

**www.woodlands-junior.kent.sch.uk/Homework/habitats.html**

For more information about endangered herbivore species, visit:

**www.endangeredspecie.com**

## Books

Chinery, Michael. *Plants and Planteaters*. Bt Bound, 2000.

Taylor, Barbara. *Plants and Animals*. Oxford: Oxford University Press, 2002.

# Glossary

**adapted:** adjusted to make suitable

**consumers:** animals that feed on plants or other animals

**cross-pollinated:** transfer of pollen from one flower to another

**deciduous:** type of tree with leaves that fall off each year

**dewlap:** the large flap of skin that hangs from a green iguana's throat

**digest:** to break down materials that can be used by the body

**endangered:** at risk of no longer living any place on Earth

**extinct:** no longer living any place on Earth

**incisors:** front teeth used for cutting and gnawing

**molars:** large teeth used for grinding food

**nectar:** a sweet liquid found in many flowers

**pollen:** a fine powder formed in flowers

**producers:** living things, such as plants, that produce their own food

**ruminants:** animals that chew cud and have more than one stomach

**savannah:** flat plain covered with grass and a few trees

**species:** a group of the same kind of living things; members can breed together

**temperate:** not too hot or too cold

**vegetation:** plant life

# Index